I0106568

Service with a Smile
"The server's handbook"

Luther T. Collins

Service with a Smile
"The Server's Handbook"

Printed in the United States of America
Published by: Legacy Voice Productions

Copyright © 2024 by Luther T. Collins

All rights reserved. This book or parts
thereof may not be reproduced in any form,
stored in a retrieval system, or transmitted in
any form by any means-electronic,
mechanical, photocopy, recording, or
otherwise-without prior written permission
of the author, except as provided by United
States of America copyright law.

ISBN 978-1-960179-13-5

To contact author for booking or ordering
additional copies, go to:
legacyvoiceproductions@gmail.com

Handbook Layout

Servant Hood

8 strategies to becoming a great server

5 Key Takeaways

Final Key Notes

My Executions

Pop Quiz

Answer Sheet

Thank you

Server Signature

Servant Hood

Being a server comes with a great responsibility that's bigger than just coming to work to see how much cash you can leave with. Serving is a lifestyle as it starts long before you enter into a building! Serving starts at home and should carry over into your employment. If you stay in a serving posture you won't have to turn it off and on like a light switch when you get to work.

What happens when you attempt to turn it on and it's not there? There's a saying that says "If you stay ready you don't have to get ready." Let this be your intentional daily attitude towards serving. **Serving is not a position but it's a posture!**

Service with a Smile
"The Server's Handbook"

8 strategies to becoming a great server

Number 1

Come in with a serving attitude. Attitude is everything as you have the ability to set the atmosphere with your actions. A serving attitude says I'm here for you. It puts others' needs before your own. It tells guests that you are not only thankful for them coming into your place of business but that you truly appreciate their business. When was the last time you genuinely told your guest thank you for coming and actually meant it? If this is not a part of your service presentation it definitely needs to be added. Your attitude should be genuine, selfless, loving, and full of gratitude.

Number 2

Your appearance is your appetizer for your customer. This simply means your uniform should be clean, pressed, and food free. Your hair should be neat and clean including facial hair. Your nails should be professional and clean as well as any visual piercings. Dirty nails, sloppy hair, a dirty apron, inappropriate tattoos, messy facial piercings, and dingy clothes may very well be a reflection of the establishment. A clean person will not eat in a dirty place. Always inspect your appearance before you serve others. You should have a smile on your face that is welcoming and inviting. Always remember your facial expression is your unofficial initial greeting.

Number 3

There is no such thing as a lazy server. I'll say it again, "There is no such thing as a lazy server!" A true server is always seeking ways to make a guest feel welcome. How would you welcome your guest at home? Cleaning tables, pre bussing tables, rolling silverware, wiping down tables and chairs, helping other servers, preparing for the next customer, etc. are all a necessary part of the service process. These things frequently go unrecognized and unnoticed but are all necessity's in the service business. This is how you properly prepare for the next guest! FYI if you are not doing these things and are indeed a lazy person than you are not a server but you are simply a fraud!

Number 4

Be accommodating and nurturing in every way possible. If your guest is in a wheelchair, make a path, open the door, move a chair, etc. If you are serving a baby or little person grab a high chair or booster seat. If you see a parent carrying a car seat offer to take the car seat but also set up the high chair to sit the baby's chair on. Be prepared to grab an extra chair or table for bigger parties. If your guests need more space don't put them in a tight area as you have to use good judgment. If you're not sure, ask as communication is the key. Never assume, never guess but always be hospitable, considerate, generous, and helpful to your guests. Open doors, go above the norm, go beyond expectations, and be neighborly to your guests. Accommodation is the breeding ground for celebration!

Number 5

Be accurate and thorough. Write down your order neatly and exactly as it was given to you. Repeat back the orders to ensure you have everything written correctly. Believe it or not your customers will appreciate you for being thorough. It's nothing worse than being hungry and having to wait only to get the wrong order because your server didn't write down your order. In the event of a mistake, be transparent with your guest and fix the error with urgency. Do not rely on your memory as this is how mistakes happen. When in doubt, write it down so you will have a record and a reference. Being quick is a plus but it means nothing without accuracy. Your ability to write, repeat, and record orders is a direct reflection of your efficiency and effectiveness. Accuracy is the new intelligence in the service world.

Number 6

Be observant and see
what the customer needs
before they say it.
Control what you can
control. Customers
should not have to ask
for refills because you
beat them to the punch.
You can't control how
fast your food comes out
but you can control how
fast you get the order in.
Always pay attention to
your guests. Your
customer should never

have to grab condiments off another table because you are attentive, available, and accessible. If your customer has to look for you it's a good chance you're not in position. Watch and wait with anticipation that more will be required. If you see a customer low on their drink, provide that refill before they run out and before they ask. It's the little things that produce WOW customer service.

Number 7

Talk to the guest if time permits, when it's slow take the time to build relationships. Be inspiring, enjoyable, funny, and have fun. When you are not busy, take time to invest in your customer. Ask them how their day is and listen for a response. Maybe they tell you they had a long day at work. Ask them what they do and sympathize with

understanding as to why
their day was long. Look
for common ground and
start a conversation.
Maybe they like sports,
maybe they travel,
maybe they are a teacher,
or maybe they may have
just lost a loved one.
Whatever the case maybe
meet them where they
are and add light, joy,
and excitement. If the
mood is high you bring
the energy. If the mood is
low you bring the
encouragement. When

you make your guests a
priority and put them
first you tell them they
are important.

Number 8

Make service an experience for each guest so much that they will desire to return. The exclamation point is when they come back and ask for you to service them. You always hear about the bad experiences more than the good. If the experience is bad it's usually amplified and has a much greater reach. However, there are some great positive experiences out there. Use this opportunity as a chance to produce a remarkable experience so much that your guests want to go and tell the world. If they remember your name and your conversation then it's a great chance you've made a customer for life. Just remember every encounter is an opportunity for excellence. Make your first impression a lasting one. Don't waste an opportunity to turn a moment into an unforgettable memory!!!

5 Key
Takeaways

Number 1

A server is a direct salesperson. Direct because you represent the brand and you are the first interactive face of the franchise. You sell yourself as a person. You sell your company as a brand. And you sell your service as a direct reflection of your establishment.

Number 2

Your attitude shows your gratitude or not. If you have a nonchalant I don't care kind of attitude you tell your guests this is just a job and I'm just here for your money. If you have an attitude of gratitude you tell your guest that you are appreciative of them and it's bigger than the tip!

Number 3

Your action determines their satisfaction. Your service matters as you can determine if a customer returns. This is a great deal of responsibility that is often overlooked and underestimated.

Number 4

Customer service is often overlooked and underbooked. Always remember the customer is not an interruption but the reason as they represent job security. The truth is people will pay and travel for great service!

Number 5

Be approachable, be presentable, be present, be attentive, be accommodating, be accessible, and be available! The customer should be comfortable addressing you. Your presentation (greeting and physical look) reflects your company's representation. Always be engaging and in the moment with the customer as you never get another opportunity to leave an initial imprint. Pay attention and look to resolve issues before they can ask for assistance (I.e. refill or spilled drink). Be welcoming and hospitable to each guest, make them feel at home. Never allow the customer to have to search for you, always stay within reach. Most importantly let the customer know you are there for them!

Final Key Notes

Treat everyone as if they tipped you $1,000.00. And don't get mad when they don't tip but smile and keep it moving as they may not have it. They may have spent their last just to get a bite to eat and get out of the cold rainy weather. That doesn't make them any less deserving of extravagant service.

For those who desire to serve, know that it's more than money. It's bigger than waiting on people but it consists of watching while you wait!

Pretend you are the guest and you're looking to be serviced! What are some of the key attributes you desire to receive when being served?

My Executions

Now that you have 8 strategies to become a great server and 5 Key Takeaways What will you do differently to ensure your guest has a better experience?

_____

_____

_____

_____

_____

_____

_____

Service with a Smile
"The Server's Handbook"

_____

_____

_____

_____

_____

_____

_____

_____

_____

_____

_____

_____

_____

_____

_____

_____

Pop Quiz

1. Is the customer always right?
2. What can you control as a server?
3. What if you don't get tipped, how do you respond?
4. What do you do if it's slow and you only have 1 table?
5. Is there such a thing as a lazy server?

Your Answers

1. _____

   _____

   _____

2. _____

   _____

   _____

3. _____

   _____

   _____

4. _____

   _____

   _____

5. _____

   _____

   _____

Answer Key

1. It's not about being right, just focus on the present experience

2. The controllables within reach i.e. the refills, how fast you get the orders in, customer accommodation, your attitude, etc.

3. You still give great service and

understand they
may not have it.
4. Build a
relationship by
talking to your
customer
5. NO, NO, NO find
something to do

Thank You

From the bottom of my heart I extend a heartfelt thank you to all of the server's who actually live, love, and serve as a lifestyle. For this is not always easy but it is very commendable and honorable.

I want to encourage you to keep being great and you will reap a great reward.

Server Agreement

I _____ agree to serve each guest to the best of my ability. I will provide great service while being accessible, accurate, available, affectionate, and assertive. I will treat each guest as I desire to be treated myself. I will not be a lazy server!

Server Signature:

_____

Thank you for taking pride in your service, now it's time to apply everything you have learned in this book going forward as it relates to being the best server you can be!

You represent the server's of the future, "Go Be Great!"

Service with a Smile
"The Server's Handbook"

www.ingramcontent.com/pod-product-compliance
Lightning Source LLC
Chambersburg PA
CBHW071752050426
42335CB00065B/1779